50 Cuban Lunch Recipes for Home

By: Kelly Johnson

Table of Contents

- Ropa Vieja
- Cuban Sandwich (Medianoche)
- Arroz con Pollo
- Picadillo
- Cuban Black Bean Soup (Sopa de Frijoles Negros)
- Vaca Frita
- Cuban-style Beef Stew (Rabo Encendido)
- Cubano Burger
- Croquetas de Jamón (Ham Croquettes)
- Tostones (Fried Green Plantains)
- Fricasé de Pollo (Chicken Fricassee)
- Cuban-style Chicken Soup (Sopa de Pollo)
- Lechón Asado (Roast Pork)
- Cuban-Style Beef Picadillo
- Masitas de Puerco (Fried Pork Chunks)
- Yuca con Mojo (Cassava with Garlic Sauce)
- Cuban-Style Shrimp Creole (Camarones Enchilados)
- Cuban Beef Empanadas
- Moros y Cristianos (Black Beans and Rice)
- Ensalada de Aguacate (Avocado Salad)
- Cuban-style Ham and Cheese Croquettes
- Pescado a la Plancha (Grilled Fish)
- Arroz Imperial (Imperial Rice)
- Cuban-style Stuffed Peppers (Pimientos Rellenos)
- Cuban-Style Beef Stuffed Potatoes (Papa Rellena)
- Cuban-Style Chicken Fricassee (Fricasé de Pollo)
- Cuban-style Meatloaf (Pulpeta)
- Cuban-Style Seafood Paella (Paella de Mariscos)
- Cuban-Style Congri (Rice and Black Beans)
- Cuban-Style Chicken and Rice (Arroz con Pollo)
- Cuban-Style Pork Chops (Chuletas de Puerco)
- Cuban-Style Black Bean Stew (Potaje de Frijoles Negros)
- Cuban-Style Chicken Salad (Ensalada de Pollo)
- Cuban-Style Stuffed Avocado (Aguacate Relleno)
- Cuban-Style Pork Sandwich (Pan con Lechón)

- Cuban-Style Fish Tacos (Tacos de Pescado)
- Cuban-Style Shrimp and Rice (Arroz con Camarones)
- Cuban-Style Beef Stir-Fry (Bistec Salteado)
- Cuban-Style Vegetable Soup (Sopa de Verduras)
- Cuban-Style Crab Cakes (Pastelitos de Cangrejo)
- Cuban-Style Beef Skewers (Pinchos de Carne)
- Cuban-Style Chicken and Plantains (Pollo con Plátanos)
- Cuban-Style Stuffed Tomatoes (Tomates Rellenos)
- Cuban-Style Seafood Salad (Ensalada de Mariscos)
- Cuban-Style Grilled Chicken (Pollo a la Parrilla)
- Cuban-Style Beef Tamales (Tamales de Carne)
- Cuban-Style Pork Stew (Cerdo en Salsa)
- Cuban-Style Stuffed Squash (Calabacitas Rellenas)
- Cuban-Style Beef Ribs (Costillas de Res)
- Cuban-Style Seafood Stew (Estofado de Mariscos)

Ropa Vieja

Ingredients:

- 2 lbs flank steak or skirt steak
- 1 onion, thinly sliced
- 1 green bell pepper, thinly sliced
- 1 red bell pepper, thinly sliced
- 3 cloves garlic, minced
- 1 can (14 oz) crushed tomatoes
- 1 cup beef broth
- 1/4 cup tomato paste
- 1 tablespoon olive oil
- 1 teaspoon ground cumin
- 1 teaspoon dried oregano
- 1 teaspoon paprika
- Salt and pepper to taste
- Chopped fresh cilantro or parsley for garnish (optional)

Instructions:

1. Season the flank steak with salt, pepper, and half of the minced garlic.
2. Heat olive oil in a large skillet or Dutch oven over medium-high heat. Sear the steak on both sides until browned, about 4-5 minutes per side. Remove the steak from the skillet and set aside.
3. In the same skillet, add the remaining minced garlic, sliced onions, and bell peppers. Cook until softened, about 5-7 minutes.
4. Stir in the crushed tomatoes, beef broth, tomato paste, cumin, oregano, and paprika. Season with salt and pepper to taste.
5. Return the seared steak to the skillet and nestle it into the sauce. Cover and simmer over low heat for 2-3 hours, or until the meat is tender and easily shreds with a fork.
6. Once the meat is tender, remove it from the skillet and shred it using two forks.
7. Return the shredded meat to the skillet and stir to combine with the sauce and vegetables. Simmer for an additional 10-15 minutes to allow the flavors to meld together.

8. Serve the Ropa Vieja hot, garnished with chopped cilantro or parsley if desired. Enjoy with rice, black beans, and fried plantains for a traditional Cuban meal.

Cuban Sandwich (Medianoche)

Ingredients:

- 1 loaf Cuban bread or French bread, cut into sandwich-sized lengths and halved horizontally
- 1/2 lb roast pork (pernil), thinly sliced
- 1/2 lb ham, thinly sliced
- 1/2 lb Swiss cheese, thinly sliced
- Dill pickles, sliced lengthwise
- Yellow mustard
- Butter or olive oil for grilling

Instructions:

1. Preheat a panini press or large skillet over medium heat.
2. Spread mustard on one half of each piece of bread.
3. Layer the bottom half of the bread with slices of roast pork, ham, Swiss cheese, and pickles.
4. Place the top half of the bread over the fillings to form a sandwich.
5. Lightly brush the outside of the sandwich with butter or olive oil.
6. Place the sandwich on the preheated panini press or skillet. If using a skillet, place a heavy pan or weight on top of the sandwich to press it down.
7. Cook the sandwich for 3-4 minutes on each side, or until the bread is crispy and the cheese is melted.
8. Remove the sandwich from the panini press or skillet and let it cool for a minute before slicing.
9. Slice the sandwich diagonally and serve hot. Enjoy your delicious homemade Cuban Sandwich!

Arroz con Pollo

Ingredients:

- 4 bone-in, skin-on chicken thighs
- 4 bone-in, skin-on chicken drumsticks
- Salt and pepper to taste
- 2 tablespoons olive oil
- 1 onion, finely chopped
- 1 bell pepper (red or green), finely chopped
- 3 cloves garlic, minced
- 1 teaspoon ground cumin
- 1 teaspoon paprika
- 1/2 teaspoon dried oregano
- 1/2 teaspoon ground turmeric
- 1 cup long-grain white rice
- 2 cups chicken broth
- 1 cup diced tomatoes (canned or fresh)
- 1 cup frozen peas
- 1/4 cup chopped fresh cilantro or parsley (for garnish)
- Lime wedges (for serving)

Instructions:

1. Season the chicken thighs and drumsticks with salt and pepper on both sides.
2. Heat olive oil in a large skillet or Dutch oven over medium-high heat. Add the chicken pieces, skin side down, and cook until golden brown, about 5 minutes per side. Remove the chicken from the skillet and set aside.
3. In the same skillet, add the chopped onion and bell pepper. Cook until softened, about 5 minutes.
4. Add the minced garlic, ground cumin, paprika, dried oregano, and ground turmeric to the skillet. Cook for another 1-2 minutes until fragrant.
5. Stir in the rice and cook for 1-2 minutes to toast the rice slightly.
6. Pour in the chicken broth and diced tomatoes. Stir to combine.
7. Return the chicken pieces to the skillet, nestling them into the rice mixture. Bring the mixture to a simmer.

8. Cover the skillet with a lid and reduce the heat to low. Cook for 20-25 minutes, or until the rice is cooked through and the chicken is tender.
9. During the last 5 minutes of cooking, add the frozen peas to the skillet and stir to incorporate.
10. Once the rice is cooked and the chicken is tender, remove the skillet from the heat. Garnish with chopped cilantro or parsley.
11. Serve the Arroz con Pollo hot, with lime wedges on the side for squeezing over the dish. Enjoy your flavorful and comforting Arroz con Pollo!

Picadillo

Ingredients:

- 1 tablespoon olive oil
- 1 onion, finely chopped
- 3 cloves garlic, minced
- 1 bell pepper (red or green), finely chopped
- 1 lb ground beef (or pork)
- 1 can (14 oz) diced tomatoes
- 2 tablespoons tomato paste
- 1/4 cup green olives, sliced
- 1/4 cup raisins
- 2 teaspoons ground cumin
- 1 teaspoon dried oregano
- 1 teaspoon paprika
- Salt and pepper to taste
- Cooked white rice, for serving
- Chopped fresh cilantro or parsley, for garnish (optional)

Instructions:

1. Heat olive oil in a large skillet over medium heat. Add the chopped onion and bell pepper. Cook until softened, about 5 minutes.
2. Add the minced garlic to the skillet and cook for another minute until fragrant.
3. Add the ground beef (or pork) to the skillet. Cook, breaking it up with a spoon, until browned and cooked through.
4. Stir in the diced tomatoes (with their juices) and tomato paste. Mix well to combine.
5. Add the sliced green olives, raisins, ground cumin, dried oregano, and paprika to the skillet. Season with salt and pepper to taste.
6. Reduce the heat to low and simmer the Picadillo for 15-20 minutes, stirring occasionally, to allow the flavors to meld together and the sauce to thicken.
7. Once the Picadillo is ready, taste and adjust the seasoning if needed.
8. Serve the Picadillo hot over cooked white rice. Garnish with chopped fresh cilantro or parsley if desired.

9. Enjoy your delicious homemade Picadillo! It's a comforting and versatile dish that pairs well with rice, beans, or tortillas.

Cuban Black Bean Soup (Sopa de Frijoles Negros)

Ingredients:

- 1 tablespoon olive oil
- 1 onion, finely chopped
- 1 bell pepper (red or green), finely chopped
- 3 cloves garlic, minced
- 2 cans (15 oz each) black beans, drained and rinsed
- 4 cups chicken or vegetable broth
- 1 teaspoon ground cumin
- 1 teaspoon dried oregano
- 1/2 teaspoon smoked paprika
- Salt and pepper to taste
- 2 bay leaves
- Juice of 1 lime
- Chopped fresh cilantro or parsley, for garnish
- Sour cream or Greek yogurt, for serving (optional)
- Sliced avocado, for serving (optional)

Instructions:

1. Heat olive oil in a large pot over medium heat. Add the chopped onion and bell pepper. Cook until softened, about 5 minutes.
2. Add the minced garlic to the pot and cook for another minute until fragrant.
3. Stir in the black beans, chicken or vegetable broth, ground cumin, dried oregano, smoked paprika, salt, pepper, and bay leaves.
4. Bring the soup to a simmer, then reduce the heat to low. Cover the pot and let the soup simmer for about 20-25 minutes to allow the flavors to meld together.
5. After simmering, remove the bay leaves from the soup.
6. Using an immersion blender or regular blender, blend the soup until smooth and creamy. Alternatively, you can leave some beans whole for texture.
7. If the soup is too thick, you can add more broth or water to reach your desired consistency.
8. Stir in the lime juice to brighten the flavors of the soup.
9. Taste and adjust the seasoning if needed.

10. Ladle the Cuban Black Bean Soup into bowls and garnish with chopped fresh cilantro or parsley.
11. Serve the soup hot, optionally topping with a dollop of sour cream or Greek yogurt and sliced avocado.
12. Enjoy your comforting and flavorful Cuban Black Bean Soup! It pairs well with crusty bread or rice on the side.

Vaca Frita

Ingredients:

- 1 lb flank steak or skirt steak, thinly sliced
- 4 cloves garlic, minced
- Juice of 2 limes
- 1 teaspoon ground cumin
- 1 teaspoon dried oregano
- Salt and pepper to taste
- 2 tablespoons olive oil
- 1 onion, thinly sliced
- 1 bell pepper (red or green), thinly sliced
- Fresh cilantro or parsley, chopped (for garnish)
- Lime wedges (for serving)

Instructions:

1. In a bowl, combine the minced garlic, lime juice, ground cumin, dried oregano, salt, and pepper. Mix well to create the marinade.
2. Place the thinly sliced steak in a shallow dish or resealable plastic bag. Pour the marinade over the steak, making sure it's evenly coated. Cover the dish or seal the bag, and marinate in the refrigerator for at least 1 hour, or overnight for best results.
3. Heat olive oil in a large skillet over medium-high heat. Add the marinated steak slices in batches, making sure not to overcrowd the pan. Cook until browned and crispy on both sides, about 3-4 minutes per side. Transfer the cooked steak to a plate and set aside.
4. In the same skillet, add the sliced onion and bell pepper. Cook until softened and caramelized, about 5-7 minutes.
5. Return the cooked steak to the skillet with the onions and bell peppers. Stir to combine and cook for an additional 2-3 minutes to heat through.
6. Remove the Vaca Frita from the skillet and transfer to a serving platter. Garnish with chopped fresh cilantro or parsley.
7. Serve the Vaca Frita hot, with lime wedges on the side for squeezing over the dish.

8. Enjoy your delicious and crispy Vaca Frita as a main dish or serve it with rice, beans, and fried plantains for a traditional Cuban meal.

Cuban-style Beef Stew (Rabo Encendido)

Ingredients:

- 3 lbs beef oxtail, cut into pieces
- Salt and pepper to taste
- 3 tablespoons olive oil
- 1 onion, finely chopped
- 1 bell pepper (red or green), finely chopped
- 4 cloves garlic, minced
- 1 can (14 oz) crushed tomatoes
- 1 cup beef broth
- 1/2 cup dry white wine
- 1 tablespoon tomato paste
- 1 tablespoon Worcestershire sauce
- 1 teaspoon ground cumin
- 1 teaspoon paprika
- 1/2 teaspoon dried oregano
- 1/2 teaspoon ground cinnamon
- 1/4 teaspoon ground cloves
- 1/4 teaspoon cayenne pepper (adjust to taste)
- 2 bay leaves
- 2 tablespoons chopped fresh cilantro or parsley (for garnish)
- Cooked white rice, for serving

Instructions:

1. Season the oxtail pieces with salt and pepper on all sides.
2. Heat olive oil in a large Dutch oven or heavy-bottomed pot over medium-high heat. Add the oxtail pieces and brown them on all sides, working in batches if necessary. Remove the browned oxtail from the pot and set aside.
3. In the same pot, add the chopped onion and bell pepper. Cook until softened, about 5 minutes.
4. Add the minced garlic to the pot and cook for another minute until fragrant.
5. Stir in the crushed tomatoes, beef broth, dry white wine, tomato paste, Worcestershire sauce, ground cumin, paprika, dried oregano, ground cinnamon, ground cloves, cayenne pepper, and bay leaves. Mix well to combine.

6. Return the browned oxtail pieces to the pot, nestling them into the sauce.
7. Bring the mixture to a simmer, then reduce the heat to low. Cover the pot and let the stew simmer gently for 2.5 to 3 hours, or until the oxtail is tender and falling off the bone. Stir occasionally and add more broth if needed to prevent the stew from drying out.
8. Once the oxtail is tender, taste the stew and adjust the seasoning if needed.
9. Remove the bay leaves from the pot.
10. Serve the Rabo Encendido hot, garnished with chopped fresh cilantro or parsley. Enjoy the stew with cooked white rice on the side to soak up the delicious sauce.
11. Store any leftovers in an airtight container in the refrigerator for up to 3 days. Reheat gently before serving.

Cubano Burger

Ingredients:

For the burger patties:

- 1 lb ground beef
- Salt and pepper to taste
- 1 teaspoon ground cumin
- 1 teaspoon dried oregano
- 1 teaspoon garlic powder
- 1 tablespoon olive oil

For assembling the burgers:

- Hamburger buns
- Sliced ham
- Swiss cheese slices
- Dill pickles, sliced lengthwise
- Yellow mustard
- Butter or olive oil for grilling

Instructions:

1. Preheat your grill or a skillet over medium-high heat.
2. In a bowl, combine the ground beef, salt, pepper, ground cumin, dried oregano, and garlic powder. Mix until well combined.
3. Divide the seasoned ground beef mixture into equal portions and shape them into burger patties.
4. Brush each burger patty with olive oil to prevent sticking.
5. Grill the burger patties for 4-5 minutes per side, or until they reach your desired level of doneness.
6. While the burgers are grilling, prepare the other ingredients. Toast the hamburger buns lightly if desired.
7. Once the burger patties are cooked, remove them from the grill and assemble the Cubano Burgers.

8. Spread mustard on the bottom half of each hamburger bun.
9. Place a burger patty on top of the mustard, followed by a slice of Swiss cheese.
10. Add a slice of ham on top of the cheese, followed by a few slices of dill pickles.
11. Place the top half of the hamburger bun on top of the pickles to complete the burger.
12. Heat a skillet or grill pan over medium heat and add a little butter or olive oil.
13. Place the assembled Cubano Burgers in the skillet or grill pan and cook for 2-3 minutes on each side, or until the cheese is melted and the buns are toasted.
14. Remove the burgers from the skillet or grill pan and serve hot.
15. Enjoy your delicious homemade Cubano Burgers with your favorite side dishes, such as fries or potato salad.

Croquetas de Jamón (Ham Croquettes)

Ingredients:

For the béchamel sauce:

- 4 tablespoons unsalted butter
- 1/4 cup all-purpose flour
- 2 cups whole milk
- Salt and pepper to taste
- 1/4 teaspoon ground nutmeg (optional)
- 1 cup finely chopped cooked ham

For breading and frying:

- 2 large eggs, beaten
- 1 cup breadcrumbs
- Vegetable oil for frying

Instructions:

1. Start by making the béchamel sauce. In a saucepan, melt the butter over medium heat.
2. Once the butter is melted, add the flour to the saucepan and whisk continuously to form a smooth paste, also known as a roux. Cook the roux for 1-2 minutes, stirring constantly.
3. Gradually pour in the milk while whisking constantly to prevent lumps from forming. Continue to cook the sauce, stirring constantly, until it thickens and coats the back of a spoon, about 5-7 minutes.
4. Season the béchamel sauce with salt, pepper, and ground nutmeg (if using). Stir in the finely chopped cooked ham and mix well to combine.
5. Transfer the béchamel mixture to a shallow dish or baking dish and spread it out evenly. Allow it to cool to room temperature, then cover with plastic wrap and refrigerate for at least 2 hours or until firm.
6. Once the béchamel mixture has chilled and firmed up, use a spoon or a small ice cream scoop to portion out small amounts of the mixture. Roll each portion into a cylindrical shape, about 2 inches long.

7. Dip each croquette into the beaten eggs, then roll it in the breadcrumbs until evenly coated. Repeat the process for all the croquettes.
8. Heat vegetable oil in a deep fryer or large skillet to 350°F (180°C).
9. Carefully add the coated croquettes to the hot oil in batches, making sure not to overcrowd the pan. Fry the croquettes for 2-3 minutes, or until golden brown and crispy.
10. Use a slotted spoon to transfer the fried croquettes to a plate lined with paper towels to drain any excess oil.
11. Serve the Croquetas de Jamón hot, garnished with a sprinkle of salt if desired. Enjoy these crispy and creamy ham croquettes as a delicious appetizer or snack!
12. You can also serve them with dipping sauces like aioli or a spicy tomato sauce.

Tostones (Fried Green Plantains)

Ingredients:

- Green (unripe) plantains
- Vegetable oil for frying
- Salt

Instructions:

1. Peel the plantains: Cut off both ends of the plantains, then use a sharp knife to make a lengthwise slit along the ridges of the plantain. Peel off the skin in sections.
2. Cut the plantains into slices: Cut the peeled plantains into slices that are about 1 to 1.5 inches thick.
3. Heat the oil: Pour enough vegetable oil into a deep skillet or frying pan to cover the bottom with about 1/2 inch of oil. Heat the oil over medium-high heat until it reaches about 350°F (175°C).
4. Fry the plantain slices: Carefully add the plantain slices to the hot oil in a single layer. Fry them for about 2-3 minutes on each side, or until they are golden brown and tender. Use a slotted spoon to transfer the fried plantain slices to a paper towel-lined plate to drain any excess oil.
5. Flatten the plantain slices: Once the fried plantain slices have cooled slightly, place each slice between two pieces of parchment paper or plastic wrap. Use the bottom of a glass or a flat object to gently flatten each slice into a thin disc, about 1/4 to 1/2 inch thick.
6. Fry the flattened plantains: Return the flattened plantain slices to the hot oil in batches. Fry them for an additional 1-2 minutes on each side, or until they are crispy and golden brown.
7. Drain and season: Once the tostones are crispy and golden brown, use a slotted spoon to transfer them to a paper towel-lined plate to drain any excess oil. Immediately sprinkle the tostones with salt while they are still hot.
8. Serve hot: Serve the tostones hot as a side dish or snack. They are delicious served with dipping sauces like garlic aioli, mojo sauce, or salsa verde.

Enjoy your crispy and savory tostones!

Fricasé de Pollo (Chicken Fricassee)

Ingredients:

- 2 lbs chicken pieces (bone-in, skin-on thighs and drumsticks are traditional)
- Salt and pepper to taste
- 2 tablespoons olive oil
- 1 onion, finely chopped
- 1 bell pepper (red or green), finely chopped
- 3 cloves garlic, minced
- 1 can (14 oz) diced tomatoes
- 1 cup chicken broth
- 1/4 cup dry white wine (optional)
- 1 teaspoon ground cumin
- 1 teaspoon dried oregano
- 1/2 teaspoon paprika
- 1 bay leaf
- 1/4 cup chopped fresh cilantro or parsley (for garnish)
- Cooked white rice, for serving

Instructions:

1. Season the chicken pieces with salt and pepper on both sides.
2. Heat olive oil in a large skillet or Dutch oven over medium-high heat. Add the chicken pieces to the skillet, skin side down, and cook until golden brown, about 4-5 minutes per side. Remove the chicken from the skillet and set aside.
3. In the same skillet, add the chopped onion and bell pepper. Cook until softened, about 5 minutes.
4. Add the minced garlic to the skillet and cook for another minute until fragrant.
5. Stir in the diced tomatoes (with their juices), chicken broth, dry white wine (if using), ground cumin, dried oregano, paprika, and bay leaf. Mix well to combine.
6. Return the chicken pieces to the skillet, nestling them into the sauce. Bring the mixture to a simmer.
7. Cover the skillet with a lid and reduce the heat to low. Let the chicken simmer gently for about 30-40 minutes, or until the chicken is cooked through and tender, and the sauce has thickened slightly. Stir occasionally.
8. Once the chicken is cooked, taste the sauce and adjust the seasoning if needed.

9. Remove the bay leaf from the skillet.
10. Serve the Chicken Fricassee hot, garnished with chopped fresh cilantro or parsley. Serve with cooked white rice on the side.
11. Enjoy your delicious homemade Fricasé de Pollo, a comforting and flavorful Cuban chicken stew!

Cuban-style Chicken Soup (Sopa de Pollo)

Ingredients:

- 1 whole chicken (about 3-4 lbs), cut into pieces
- Salt and pepper to taste
- 2 tablespoons olive oil
- 1 onion, finely chopped
- 2 carrots, peeled and diced
- 2 celery stalks, diced
- 3 cloves garlic, minced
- 1 bell pepper (red or green), diced
- 1 can (14 oz) diced tomatoes
- 8 cups chicken broth
- 1 teaspoon ground cumin
- 1 teaspoon dried oregano
- 1/2 teaspoon paprika
- 1 bay leaf
- 1 cup frozen corn kernels
- 1 cup frozen green peas
- 1/4 cup chopped fresh cilantro or parsley (for garnish)
- Lime wedges (for serving)
- Cooked white rice (optional, for serving)

Instructions:

1. Season the chicken pieces with salt and pepper on both sides.
2. Heat olive oil in a large pot or Dutch oven over medium-high heat. Add the chicken pieces to the pot and brown them on all sides, about 4-5 minutes per side. Remove the chicken from the pot and set aside.
3. In the same pot, add the chopped onion, carrots, celery, garlic, and bell pepper. Cook until the vegetables are softened, about 5-7 minutes.
4. Stir in the diced tomatoes (with their juices), chicken broth, ground cumin, dried oregano, paprika, and bay leaf. Mix well to combine.
5. Return the browned chicken pieces to the pot, nestling them into the broth and vegetables. Bring the soup to a simmer.

6. Cover the pot with a lid and reduce the heat to low. Let the soup simmer gently for about 45-60 minutes, or until the chicken is cooked through and tender.
7. Once the chicken is cooked, remove it from the pot and shred the meat using two forks. Discard the bones and return the shredded chicken to the pot.
8. Stir in the frozen corn kernels and green peas. Let the soup simmer for an additional 5-10 minutes, or until the vegetables are heated through.
9. Taste the soup and adjust the seasoning if needed.
10. Serve the Cuban-style Chicken Soup hot, garnished with chopped fresh cilantro or parsley. Serve with lime wedges on the side for squeezing over the soup. You can also serve the soup with cooked white rice on the side, if desired.
11. Enjoy your comforting and flavorful Sopa de Pollo!

Lechón Asado (Roast Pork)

Ingredients:

- 1 whole pork shoulder or pork leg (about 6-8 lbs), skin-on
- 8 cloves garlic, minced
- Juice of 2 oranges
- Juice of 2 limes
- 1/4 cup olive oil
- 2 tablespoons white vinegar
- 2 teaspoons dried oregano
- 2 teaspoons ground cumin
- 2 teaspoons paprika
- 2 teaspoons salt
- 1 teaspoon black pepper
- 1 onion, thinly sliced
- 1 bell pepper (red or green), thinly sliced
- 1 cup chicken broth or water

Instructions:

1. Using a sharp knife, score the skin of the pork shoulder or leg with shallow cuts, being careful not to cut too deeply into the meat.
2. In a bowl, combine the minced garlic, orange juice, lime juice, olive oil, white vinegar, dried oregano, ground cumin, paprika, salt, and black pepper. Mix well to create the marinade.
3. Place the pork in a large resealable plastic bag or a shallow dish. Pour the marinade over the pork, making sure it's evenly coated. Add the sliced onion and bell pepper to the bag or dish. Seal the bag or cover the dish, and refrigerate the pork to marinate for at least 4 hours, or preferably overnight.
4. Preheat your oven to 325°F (165°C).
5. Remove the marinated pork from the refrigerator and let it come to room temperature for about 30 minutes before roasting.
6. Transfer the pork and marinade to a roasting pan or baking dish, making sure the pork is placed skin-side up. Pour the chicken broth or water into the bottom of the pan.

7. Cover the pan tightly with aluminum foil and roast the pork in the preheated oven for about 3-4 hours, or until the meat is very tender and easily pulls apart with a fork.
8. Remove the foil from the pan and increase the oven temperature to 450°F (230°C). Return the pork to the oven and roast for an additional 30-45 minutes, or until the skin is crispy and golden brown.
9. Once the Lechón Asado is done, remove it from the oven and let it rest for about 15 minutes before carving.
10. Carve the roast pork into slices or chunks, and serve it hot with the cooked onions, bell peppers, and pan juices spooned over the top.
11. Enjoy your delicious homemade Lechón Asado, a classic Cuban dish that's perfect for special occasions and gatherings!

Cuban-Style Beef Picadillo

Ingredients:

- 1 lb ground beef
- 1 tablespoon olive oil
- 1 onion, finely chopped
- 1 bell pepper (red or green), finely chopped
- 3 cloves garlic, minced
- 1 can (14 oz) diced tomatoes
- 1/4 cup tomato sauce
- 1/4 cup beef broth or water
- 1/4 cup green olives, sliced
- 1/4 cup raisins
- 2 teaspoons ground cumin
- 1 teaspoon dried oregano
- 1/2 teaspoon paprika
- Salt and pepper to taste
- Cooked white rice, for serving
- Chopped fresh cilantro or parsley, for garnish (optional)

Instructions:

1. Heat olive oil in a large skillet over medium heat. Add the chopped onion and bell pepper. Cook until softened, about 5 minutes.
2. Add the minced garlic to the skillet and cook for another minute until fragrant.
3. Add the ground beef to the skillet. Cook, breaking it up with a spoon, until browned and cooked through.
4. Stir in the diced tomatoes (with their juices), tomato sauce, beef broth (or water), green olives, raisins, ground cumin, dried oregano, paprika, salt, and pepper. Mix well to combine.
5. Bring the mixture to a simmer, then reduce the heat to low. Cover the skillet and let the picadillo simmer for about 20-25 minutes, stirring occasionally, to allow the flavors to meld together and the sauce to thicken.
6. Taste the picadillo and adjust the seasoning if needed.
7. Serve the Cuban-style beef picadillo hot over cooked white rice. Garnish with chopped fresh cilantro or parsley if desired.

8. Enjoy your delicious homemade Cuban-style beef picadillo! It's a comforting and satisfying dish that's perfect for weeknight dinners.

Masitas de Puerco (Fried Pork Chunks)

Ingredients:

- 2 lbs pork shoulder, cut into bite-sized chunks
- 8 cloves garlic, minced
- Juice of 2 oranges
- Juice of 2 limes
- 1 teaspoon ground cumin
- 1 teaspoon dried oregano
- 1 teaspoon paprika
- 1 teaspoon salt
- 1/2 teaspoon black pepper
- Vegetable oil for frying

Instructions:

1. In a large bowl, combine the minced garlic, orange juice, lime juice, ground cumin, dried oregano, paprika, salt, and black pepper. Mix well to create the marinade.
2. Add the pork chunks to the marinade, making sure they are evenly coated. Cover the bowl and refrigerate for at least 2 hours, or overnight for best results.
3. Remove the marinated pork from the refrigerator and let it come to room temperature for about 30 minutes before frying.
4. Heat vegetable oil in a deep skillet or frying pan over medium-high heat until it reaches about 350°F (175°C).
5. Carefully add the marinated pork chunks to the hot oil in batches, making sure not to overcrowd the pan. Fry the pork chunks for about 5-7 minutes per batch, or until they are golden brown and crispy on all sides.
6. Use a slotted spoon to transfer the fried pork chunks to a plate lined with paper towels to drain any excess oil.
7. Serve the Masitas de Puerco hot as a delicious appetizer or main dish. They pair well with rice, beans, and fried plantains.
8. Enjoy your crispy and flavorful Masitas de Puerco!

Yuca con Mojo (Cassava with Garlic Sauce)

Ingredients:

For the Yuca:

- 2 lbs yuca (cassava), peeled and cut into chunks
- Water
- Salt

For the Mojo Sauce:

- 1/2 cup olive oil
- 8 cloves garlic, minced
- Juice of 2-3 sour oranges or substitute with a mixture of lime and orange juice
- 1 teaspoon dried oregano
- Salt and pepper to taste
- Chopped fresh cilantro or parsley for garnish (optional)

Instructions:

1. Prepare the Yuca:
    - Peel the yuca and cut it into large chunks, discarding any woody core in the center.
    - Place the yuca chunks in a large pot and cover them with water. Add a generous pinch of salt to the water.
    - Bring the water to a boil over medium-high heat, then reduce the heat to medium-low and let the yuca simmer for about 20-25 minutes, or until it is tender when pierced with a fork.
    - Drain the cooked yuca and set it aside.
2. Make the Mojo Sauce:
    - In a small saucepan, heat the olive oil over medium heat. Add the minced garlic and cook, stirring constantly, for about 1-2 minutes, or until the garlic is fragrant and just beginning to turn golden brown.
    - Remove the saucepan from the heat and carefully add the sour orange juice (or lime and orange juice mixture) to the garlic and oil. Be cautious, as the mixture may sizzle.

- Stir in the dried oregano and season with salt and pepper to taste. Mix well to combine.
- Set the mojo sauce aside and let it cool slightly.
3. Serve:
    - Arrange the cooked yuca on a serving platter or individual plates.
    - Pour the warm mojo sauce over the yuca, making sure to evenly distribute it.
    - Garnish the yuca con mojo with chopped fresh cilantro or parsley, if desired.
    - Serve the dish warm as a side dish or appetizer.
4. Enjoy your delicious Yuca con Mojo! This dish is perfect for sharing with family and friends, and it pairs well with grilled meats, rice, beans, or fried plantains.

Cuban-Style Shrimp Creole (Camarones Enchilados)

Ingredients:

- 1 lb large shrimp, peeled and deveined
- Salt and pepper to taste
- 2 tablespoons olive oil
- 1 onion, finely chopped
- 1 bell pepper (red or green), finely chopped
- 3 cloves garlic, minced
- 1 can (14 oz) diced tomatoes
- 1/2 cup tomato sauce
- 1/4 cup white wine (optional)
- 1 teaspoon ground cumin
- 1 teaspoon paprika
- 1/2 teaspoon dried oregano
- 1/4 teaspoon cayenne pepper (adjust to taste)
- 1 bay leaf
- Chopped fresh cilantro or parsley for garnish
- Cooked white rice for serving

Instructions:

1. Season the shrimp with salt and pepper to taste and set aside.
2. Heat olive oil in a large skillet or Dutch oven over medium heat. Add the chopped onion and bell pepper. Cook until softened, about 5 minutes.
3. Add the minced garlic to the skillet and cook for another minute until fragrant.
4. Stir in the diced tomatoes (with their juices), tomato sauce, white wine (if using), ground cumin, paprika, dried oregano, cayenne pepper, and bay leaf. Mix well to combine.
5. Bring the sauce to a simmer and let it cook for about 10 minutes to allow the flavors to meld together and the sauce to thicken slightly.
6. Add the seasoned shrimp to the skillet and stir to coat them with the sauce.
7. Cover the skillet and let the shrimp cook for about 5-7 minutes, or until they are pink and cooked through.
8. Once the shrimp are cooked, taste the sauce and adjust the seasoning if needed.
9. Remove the bay leaf from the skillet and discard.

10. Serve the Camarones Enchilados hot, garnished with chopped fresh cilantro or parsley. Serve with cooked white rice on the side.
11. Enjoy your delicious Cuban-style Shrimp Creole! It's a flavorful and satisfying dish that's perfect for weeknight dinners or special occasions.

Cuban Beef Empanadas

Ingredients:

For the dough:

- 2 cups all-purpose flour
- 1/2 teaspoon salt
- 1/2 cup (1 stick) unsalted butter, cold and cut into cubes
- 1 large egg
- 1/4 cup cold water

For the filling:

- 1 tablespoon olive oil
- 1 onion, finely chopped
- 1 bell pepper (red or green), finely chopped
- 2 cloves garlic, minced
- 1 lb ground beef
- 1 teaspoon ground cumin
- 1 teaspoon paprika
- 1/2 teaspoon dried oregano
- Salt and pepper to taste
- 1/4 cup tomato sauce
- 2 tablespoons chopped fresh cilantro or parsley
- 1/4 cup pitted green olives, sliced (optional)
- 1/4 cup raisins (optional)

For assembling and finishing:

- 1 egg, beaten (for egg wash)
- Sesame seeds (optional, for sprinkling)

Instructions:

1. Make the dough:
    - In a large mixing bowl, combine the flour and salt. Add the cold cubed butter and use your fingers or a pastry cutter to work the butter into the flour until the mixture resembles coarse crumbs.
    - In a small bowl, whisk together the egg and cold water. Pour the egg mixture into the flour mixture and stir until the dough comes together.
    - Turn the dough out onto a lightly floured surface and knead gently until smooth. Wrap the dough in plastic wrap and refrigerate for at least 30 minutes.
2. Make the filling:
    - Heat olive oil in a large skillet over medium heat. Add the chopped onion and bell pepper. Cook until softened, about 5 minutes.
    - Add the minced garlic to the skillet and cook for another minute until fragrant.
    - Add the ground beef to the skillet, breaking it up with a spoon. Cook until browned and cooked through.
    - Stir in the ground cumin, paprika, dried oregano, salt, and pepper. Cook for another minute to toast the spices.
    - Add the tomato sauce, chopped cilantro or parsley, green olives (if using), and raisins (if using). Mix well to combine. Remove the skillet from the heat and let the filling cool slightly.
3. Preheat your oven to 375°F (190°C). Line a baking sheet with parchment paper.
4. Assemble the empanadas:
    - On a lightly floured surface, roll out the chilled dough to about 1/8 inch thickness. Use a round cutter or a small plate to cut out circles of dough, about 4-6 inches in diameter.
    - Place a spoonful of the beef filling in the center of each dough circle. Fold the dough over the filling to form a half-moon shape. Press the edges together to seal, then crimp with a fork to create a decorative edge.
    - Place the assembled empanadas on the prepared baking sheet. Brush the tops with beaten egg and sprinkle with sesame seeds, if desired.
5. Bake the empanadas:
    - Bake in the preheated oven for 20-25 minutes, or until the empanadas are golden brown and crispy.
6. Serve the Cuban Beef Empanadas hot or at room temperature, with your favorite dipping sauce or salsa on the side.
7. Enjoy your homemade Cuban Beef Empanadas as a delicious appetizer, snack, or main dish!

Moros y Cristianos (Black Beans and Rice)

Ingredients:

For the black beans:

- 1 cup dried black beans
- Water for soaking and cooking
- 1 tablespoon olive oil
- 1 onion, finely chopped
- 1 bell pepper (red or green), finely chopped
- 3 cloves garlic, minced
- 1 teaspoon ground cumin
- 1 teaspoon dried oregano
- 1 bay leaf
- Salt and pepper to taste

For the rice:

- 1 cup long-grain white rice
- 2 cups water or chicken broth
- Salt to taste

Instructions:

1. Prepare the black beans:
    - Rinse the dried black beans under cold water and remove any debris. Place the beans in a large bowl and cover them with water. Let them soak overnight, or for at least 8 hours.
    - After soaking, drain and rinse the beans again.
    - In a large pot, heat olive oil over medium heat. Add the chopped onion and bell pepper. Cook until softened, about 5 minutes.
    - Add the minced garlic to the pot and cook for another minute until fragrant.
    - Stir in the soaked black beans, ground cumin, dried oregano, bay leaf, and enough water to cover the beans by about 2 inches.

- Bring the mixture to a boil, then reduce the heat to low. Cover the pot and let the beans simmer gently for 1 to 1.5 hours, or until the beans are tender. Stir occasionally and add more water if needed to prevent the beans from drying out.
- Once the beans are tender, season them with salt and pepper to taste. Remove the bay leaf and discard.

2. Prepare the rice:
    - In a separate pot, combine the rice and water or chicken broth. Add salt to taste.
    - Bring the mixture to a boil, then reduce the heat to low. Cover the pot and let the rice simmer for 18-20 minutes, or until the rice is tender and the liquid is absorbed.
    - Once the rice is cooked, fluff it with a fork and remove it from the heat.
3. Combine the beans and rice:
    - Once both the beans and rice are cooked, combine them in a large serving bowl or pot.
    - Mix the beans and rice together gently until well combined.
4. Serve:
    - Serve Moros y Cristianos hot as a side dish or main course.
    - Garnish with chopped fresh cilantro or parsley, if desired.
    - Enjoy your delicious homemade Moros y Cristianos!

Ensalada de Aguacate (Avocado Salad)

Ingredients:

- 2 ripe avocados, peeled, pitted, and sliced
- 1 large tomato, sliced
- 1/2 red onion, thinly sliced
- 1/4 cup chopped fresh cilantro
- Juice of 1 lime
- 2 tablespoons extra-virgin olive oil
- Salt and pepper to taste

Instructions:

1. In a large serving bowl, arrange the sliced avocado, tomato, and red onion.
2. Sprinkle the chopped cilantro over the top of the salad ingredients.
3. Drizzle the lime juice and olive oil over the salad.
4. Season the salad with salt and pepper to taste.
5. Gently toss the salad ingredients together until evenly coated with the lime juice, olive oil, and seasonings.
6. Serve the Ensalada de Aguacate immediately as a refreshing side dish or appetizer.
7. Enjoy the creamy texture and vibrant flavors of this delicious Avocado Salad!

Feel free to customize this salad by adding additional ingredients such as diced cucumber, bell pepper, or radishes. You can also adjust the seasonings to suit your taste preferences.

Cuban-style Ham and Cheese Croquettes

Ingredients:

For the croquettes:

- 4 tablespoons unsalted butter
- 1/4 cup all-purpose flour
- 2 cups whole milk
- Salt and pepper to taste
- 1/4 teaspoon ground nutmeg (optional)
- 1 cup finely chopped cooked ham
- 1 cup shredded cheese (such as Swiss or Gruyere)
- 2 eggs, beaten
- 1 cup breadcrumbs
- Vegetable oil for frying

For serving:

- Dipping sauce of your choice (e.g., mustard, aioli, or tomato sauce)

Instructions:

1. Prepare the béchamel sauce:
    - In a saucepan, melt the butter over medium heat.
    - Once melted, add the flour and whisk continuously to form a smooth paste (roux). Cook the roux for 1-2 minutes, stirring constantly.
    - Gradually pour in the milk while whisking constantly to prevent lumps from forming. Continue to cook the sauce, stirring constantly, until it thickens and coats the back of a spoon, about 5-7 minutes.
    - Season the béchamel sauce with salt, pepper, and ground nutmeg (if using). Stir in the finely chopped cooked ham and shredded cheese. Mix well until the cheese is melted and the ingredients are evenly combined.
    - Transfer the mixture to a shallow dish or baking dish and spread it out evenly. Allow it to cool to room temperature, then cover with plastic wrap and refrigerate for at least 2 hours or until firm.
2. Shape and coat the croquettes:

- Once the béchamel mixture has chilled and firmed up, use a spoon or a small ice cream scoop to portion out small amounts of the mixture. Roll each portion into a cylindrical shape, about 2 inches long.
- Dip each croquette into the beaten eggs, then roll it in the breadcrumbs until evenly coated. Repeat the process for all the croquettes.

3. Fry the croquettes:
   - Heat vegetable oil in a deep fryer or large skillet to 350°F (180°C).
   - Carefully add the coated croquettes to the hot oil in batches, making sure not to overcrowd the pan. Fry the croquettes for 2-3 minutes, or until golden brown and crispy.
   - Use a slotted spoon to transfer the fried croquettes to a plate lined with paper towels to drain any excess oil.
4. Serve:
   - Serve the Cuban-style Ham and Cheese Croquettes hot, accompanied by your favorite dipping sauce.
   - Enjoy these crispy and creamy croquettes as a delicious appetizer or snack!

Feel free to customize the croquettes by adding additional ingredients such as chopped herbs, spices, or different types of cheese.

Pescado a la Plancha (Grilled Fish)

Ingredients:

- 4 fillets of firm white fish (such as tilapia, snapper, or cod)
- Salt and pepper to taste
- 2 tablespoons olive oil
- 2 cloves garlic, minced
- Juice of 1 lemon
- Chopped fresh parsley for garnish (optional)
- Lemon wedges for serving

Instructions:

1. Preheat your grill or griddle to medium-high heat. Make sure the surface is clean and lightly oiled to prevent the fish from sticking.
2. Pat the fish fillets dry with paper towels and season them generously with salt and pepper on both sides.
3. In a small bowl, mix together the olive oil, minced garlic, and lemon juice to create a marinade.
4. Brush the marinade over the fish fillets, making sure to coat them evenly.
5. Place the seasoned fish fillets on the preheated grill or griddle. Cook for about 3-4 minutes on each side, depending on the thickness of the fillets, or until the fish is opaque and flakes easily with a fork.
6. While grilling, avoid flipping the fish too often to prevent it from sticking and to allow it to develop a nice char.
7. Once the fish is cooked through and has a golden-brown crust, remove it from the grill or griddle.
8. Transfer the grilled fish fillets to a serving platter and garnish with chopped fresh parsley, if desired.
9. Serve the Pescado a la Plancha hot, accompanied by lemon wedges on the side for squeezing over the fish.
10. Enjoy your flavorful and tender Grilled Fish as a healthy and satisfying main dish!

Feel free to customize the seasoning for the fish by adding your favorite herbs, spices, or marinades. Additionally, you can serve the grilled fish with a side of rice, vegetables, or a fresh salad for a complete meal.

Arroz Imperial (Imperial Rice)

Ingredients:

For the chicken:

- 2 boneless, skinless chicken breasts
- 2 cloves garlic, minced
- 1 teaspoon ground cumin
- 1 teaspoon dried oregano
- Salt and pepper to taste
- 1 tablespoon olive oil
- Water or chicken broth for cooking

For the rice:

- 2 cups long-grain white rice
- 4 cups water or chicken broth
- Salt to taste
- 2 tablespoons unsalted butter

For assembling:

- 1 cup mayonnaise
- 1 cup grated cheese (such as Swiss or Gouda)
- Sliced pimientos or roasted red peppers for garnish (optional)
- Chopped fresh parsley for garnish (optional)

Instructions:

1. Prepare the chicken:
    - Season the chicken breasts with minced garlic, ground cumin, dried oregano, salt, and pepper.

- Heat olive oil in a skillet over medium-high heat. Add the seasoned chicken breasts and cook until golden brown on both sides, about 4-5 minutes per side.
- Add enough water or chicken broth to the skillet to cover the chicken breasts halfway. Reduce the heat to medium-low, cover the skillet, and simmer until the chicken is cooked through, about 15-20 minutes.
- Once cooked, remove the chicken from the skillet and let it cool slightly. Shred the chicken into bite-sized pieces using two forks. Set aside.

2. Prepare the rice:
   - In a large saucepan, combine the rice and water or chicken broth. Add salt to taste.
   - Bring the mixture to a boil over medium-high heat, then reduce the heat to low. Cover the saucepan and let the rice simmer for 18-20 minutes, or until the rice is tender and the liquid is absorbed.
   - Once cooked, fluff the rice with a fork and stir in the unsalted butter until melted. Set aside.

3. Assemble the Arroz Imperial:
   - Preheat your oven to 375°F (190°C). Lightly grease a baking dish with cooking spray or butter.
   - Spread half of the cooked rice evenly in the bottom of the prepared baking dish.
   - Top the rice layer with the shredded chicken, spreading it out evenly.
   - Spread the mayonnaise over the chicken layer, covering it completely.
   - Sprinkle the grated cheese evenly over the mayonnaise layer.
   - Top the cheese layer with the remaining cooked rice, spreading it out evenly.

4. Bake the Arroz Imperial:
   - Place the assembled dish in the preheated oven and bake for 25-30 minutes, or until the top is golden brown and bubbly.
   - Once baked, remove the Arroz Imperial from the oven and let it cool for a few minutes before serving.

5. Serve the Arroz Imperial hot, garnished with sliced pimientos or roasted red peppers and chopped fresh parsley, if desired.

6. Enjoy your delicious Arroz Imperial as a comforting and flavorful main dish or side dish!

Cuban-style Stuffed Peppers (Pimientos Rellenos)

Ingredients:

- 4 large bell peppers (any color), halved and seeds removed
- 1 lb ground beef
- 1 onion, finely chopped
- 2 cloves garlic, minced
- 1 tomato, diced
- 1/2 cup cooked rice
- 1 teaspoon ground cumin
- 1 teaspoon paprika
- 1/2 teaspoon dried oregano
- Salt and pepper to taste
- 1 cup tomato sauce
- 1 cup shredded cheese (such as mozzarella or cheddar)
- Chopped fresh cilantro or parsley for garnish (optional)

Instructions:

1. Preheat your oven to 375°F (190°C). Lightly grease a baking dish with cooking spray or olive oil.
2. In a large skillet, cook the ground beef over medium heat until browned and cooked through, breaking it up with a spoon as it cooks.
3. Add the chopped onion and minced garlic to the skillet with the cooked ground beef. Cook for another 3-4 minutes, or until the onion is softened and translucent.
4. Stir in the diced tomato, cooked rice, ground cumin, paprika, dried oregano, salt, and pepper. Cook for another 2-3 minutes to allow the flavors to meld together. Remove the skillet from the heat.
5. Spoon the beef and rice mixture into each halved bell pepper, filling them evenly.
6. Place the stuffed bell peppers in the prepared baking dish. Pour the tomato sauce over the stuffed peppers, covering them evenly.
7. Cover the baking dish with aluminum foil and bake in the preheated oven for 25-30 minutes, or until the peppers are tender.
8. Remove the foil from the baking dish and sprinkle the shredded cheese over the tops of the stuffed peppers.

9. Return the baking dish to the oven and bake for an additional 5-7 minutes, or until the cheese is melted and bubbly.
10. Once baked, remove the stuffed peppers from the oven and let them cool for a few minutes before serving.
11. Garnish the Cuban-style Stuffed Peppers with chopped fresh cilantro or parsley, if desired.
12. Serve the stuffed peppers hot as a delicious and comforting main dish or side dish.
13. Enjoy your flavorful and satisfying Pimientos Rellenos!

Cuban-Style Beef Stuffed Potatoes (Papa Rellena)

Ingredients:

For the potato dough:

- 4 large russet potatoes, peeled and diced
- Salt to taste
- 2 tablespoons unsalted butter
- 1/4 cup milk
- 1 egg, beaten
- 1/2 cup all-purpose flour (for coating)

For the beef filling:

- 1 tablespoon olive oil
- 1 onion, finely chopped
- 2 cloves garlic, minced
- 1 lb ground beef
- 1 teaspoon ground cumin
- 1 teaspoon paprika
- 1/2 teaspoon dried oregano
- Salt and pepper to taste
- 1/4 cup tomato sauce
- 1/4 cup green olives, chopped
- 2 hard-boiled eggs, chopped

For frying:

- Vegetable oil for deep frying

Instructions:

1. Prepare the potato dough:
    - Place the diced potatoes in a large pot of salted water. Bring the water to a boil and cook the potatoes until tender, about 15-20 minutes.

- Drain the cooked potatoes and return them to the pot. Mash the potatoes with a potato masher or fork until smooth.
- Add the unsalted butter and milk to the mashed potatoes, and mix until well combined and creamy. Season with salt to taste.
- Let the mashed potatoes cool slightly, then stir in the beaten egg until fully incorporated.

2. Prepare the beef filling:
   - In a large skillet, heat olive oil over medium heat. Add the chopped onion and minced garlic, and cook until softened, about 5 minutes.
   - Add the ground beef to the skillet, breaking it up with a spoon. Cook until browned and cooked through.
   - Stir in the ground cumin, paprika, dried oregano, salt, and pepper. Cook for another minute to toast the spices.
   - Add the tomato sauce, chopped green olives, and chopped hard-boiled eggs to the skillet. Mix well to combine. Remove the skillet from the heat and let the filling cool slightly.
3. Assemble the Papa Rellena:
   - Take a small portion of the mashed potato dough and flatten it in the palm of your hand. Place a spoonful of the beef filling in the center of the flattened potato dough.
   - Carefully fold the potato dough around the filling, shaping it into a smooth ball. Repeat the process with the remaining potato dough and beef filling.
4. Coat and fry the Papa Rellena:
   - Roll each stuffed potato ball in flour until evenly coated, shaking off any excess flour.
   - Heat vegetable oil in a deep fryer or large pot to 350°F (175°C).
   - Carefully add the coated potato balls to the hot oil in batches, making sure not to overcrowd the pot. Fry the Papa Rellena for 3-4 minutes, or until golden brown and crispy.
   - Use a slotted spoon to transfer the fried Papa Rellena to a plate lined with paper towels to drain any excess oil.
5. Serve the Papa Rellena hot as a delicious appetizer or main dish.
6. Enjoy your flavorful and crispy Cuban-style Beef Stuffed Potatoes!

Cuban-Style Chicken Fricassee (Fricasé de Pollo)

Ingredients:

- 2 lbs chicken pieces (such as thighs, drumsticks, or breasts), skin-on and bone-in
- Salt and pepper to taste
- 2 tablespoons olive oil
- 1 onion, finely chopped
- 1 bell pepper (red or green), finely chopped
- 2 cloves garlic, minced
- 1 tomato, diced
- 1/4 cup dry white wine (optional)
- 1 cup chicken broth
- 1/4 teaspoon ground cumin
- 1/2 teaspoon dried oregano
- 1 bay leaf
- 1/4 cup pitted green olives, sliced
- 2 tablespoons capers, drained
- 1 tablespoon tomato paste
- 1 tablespoon all-purpose flour (optional, for thickening)
- Chopped fresh cilantro or parsley for garnish (optional)

Instructions:

1. Season the chicken pieces generously with salt and pepper on both sides.
2. In a large skillet or Dutch oven, heat olive oil over medium-high heat. Add the chicken pieces to the skillet and brown them on all sides, about 5-7 minutes per side. Remove the chicken from the skillet and set it aside.
3. In the same skillet, add the chopped onion and bell pepper. Cook until softened, about 5 minutes.
4. Add the minced garlic to the skillet and cook for another minute until fragrant.
5. Stir in the diced tomato and cook for 2-3 minutes until softened.
6. Pour in the dry white wine (if using) to deglaze the skillet, scraping up any browned bits from the bottom.
7. Return the browned chicken pieces to the skillet, along with any accumulated juices.

8. Add the chicken broth, ground cumin, dried oregano, and bay leaf to the skillet. Bring the mixture to a simmer.
9. Cover the skillet and let the chicken simmer over medium-low heat for about 30 minutes, or until the chicken is cooked through and tender.
10. Stir in the sliced green olives, drained capers, and tomato paste. Mix well to combine.
11. If you prefer a thicker sauce, you can make a slurry by mixing the flour with a little water until smooth, then stir it into the sauce. Cook for a few more minutes until the sauce thickens slightly.
12. Taste the sauce and adjust the seasoning with salt and pepper if needed.
13. Once the chicken is cooked and the sauce is thickened to your liking, remove the skillet from the heat.
14. Garnish the Cuban-Style Chicken Fricassee with chopped fresh cilantro or parsley, if desired.
15. Serve the Fricasé de Pollo hot, accompanied by rice, mashed potatoes, or crusty bread to soak up the delicious sauce.
16. Enjoy your flavorful and comforting Cuban-style Chicken Fricassee!

Cuban-style Meatloaf (Pulpeta)

Ingredients:

For the meatloaf:

- 1 lb ground beef (you can also use a mixture of ground beef and pork)
- 1 onion, finely chopped
- 1 bell pepper (red or green), finely chopped
- 2 cloves garlic, minced
- 1/2 cup breadcrumbs
- 1/4 cup milk
- 2 eggs, beaten
- 1 teaspoon ground cumin
- 1 teaspoon dried oregano
- 1/2 teaspoon paprika
- Salt and pepper to taste

For the glaze:

- 1/4 cup ketchup
- 2 tablespoons brown sugar
- 1 tablespoon Worcestershire sauce
- 1 tablespoon apple cider vinegar

Instructions:

1. Preheat your oven to 350°F (175°C). Lightly grease a loaf pan with cooking spray or olive oil.
2. In a large mixing bowl, combine the ground beef, chopped onion, chopped bell pepper, minced garlic, breadcrumbs, milk, beaten eggs, ground cumin, dried oregano, paprika, salt, and pepper. Mix well until all ingredients are evenly combined.
3. Transfer the meatloaf mixture to the prepared loaf pan and use your hands to shape it into a loaf shape, pressing it down firmly to compact it.

4. In a small bowl, whisk together the ketchup, brown sugar, Worcestershire sauce, and apple cider vinegar to make the glaze.
5. Spread the glaze evenly over the top of the meatloaf, using a spoon or pastry brush to coat it completely.
6. Place the meatloaf in the preheated oven and bake for 50-60 minutes, or until the meatloaf is cooked through and the internal temperature reaches 160°F (71°C).
7. Once baked, remove the meatloaf from the oven and let it rest for 5-10 minutes before slicing.
8. Slice the Cuban-style Meatloaf (Pulpeta) and serve it hot, garnished with chopped fresh parsley or cilantro if desired.
9. Enjoy your flavorful and comforting Pulpeta as a delicious main dish, accompanied by mashed potatoes, rice, or your favorite side dishes.
10. Leftovers can be stored in an airtight container in the refrigerator for up to 3 days.

Cuban-Style Seafood Paella (Paella de Mariscos)

Ingredients:

- 1 lb mixed seafood (such as shrimp, squid, mussels, and clams)
- 2 cups bomba or Arborio rice
- 4 cups seafood or chicken broth
- 1 onion, diced
- 1 bell pepper (red or green), diced
- 2 cloves garlic, minced
- 1 tomato, diced
- 1/2 cup frozen peas
- 1/4 cup chopped parsley
- 1 lemon, cut into wedges
- 1/4 cup olive oil
- Salt and pepper to taste
- 1 teaspoon smoked paprika
- 1/2 teaspoon saffron threads
- 1/2 cup dry white wine
- Lemon wedges, for serving

Instructions:

1. Heat the olive oil in a large paella pan or skillet over medium heat. Add the diced onion and bell pepper, and cook until softened, about 5 minutes.
2. Add the minced garlic and diced tomato to the pan, and cook for another 2-3 minutes.
3. Stir in the rice, smoked paprika, and saffron threads, and cook for 1-2 minutes, stirring constantly.
4. Pour in the dry white wine, and cook until it has evaporated, stirring occasionally.
5. Add the seafood or chicken broth to the pan, and season with salt and pepper to taste. Bring the mixture to a simmer.
6. Reduce the heat to low, and let the rice cook uncovered for about 15-20 minutes, or until most of the liquid has been absorbed and the rice is almost tender.
7. While the rice is cooking, prepare the seafood. If using clams and mussels, make sure to clean and debeard them. Peel and devein the shrimp, and clean the squid.

8. Once the rice is almost tender, add the mixed seafood to the pan, nestling it into the rice. Arrange the clams and mussels on top of the rice, making sure they are tightly closed.
9. Scatter the frozen peas over the top of the paella, cover the pan with a lid or aluminum foil, and let it cook for another 5-10 minutes, or until the seafood is cooked through and the clams and mussels have opened.
10. Remove the paella from the heat, and sprinkle the chopped parsley over the top. Serve the Cuban-Style Seafood Paella hot, garnished with lemon wedges for squeezing over the paella.
11. Enjoy your flavorful and aromatic Paella de Mariscos, reminiscent of Cuban cuisine!

Cuban-Style Congri (Rice and Black Beans)

Ingredients:

- 1 cup long-grain white rice
- 1 cup dried black beans
- 4 cups water
- 2 tablespoons olive oil
- 1 onion, finely chopped
- 1 bell pepper (red or green), finely chopped
- 3 cloves garlic, minced
- 1 teaspoon ground cumin
- 1 teaspoon dried oregano
- Salt and pepper to taste
- 1 bay leaf
- 2 tablespoons tomato paste
- 2 tablespoons chopped fresh cilantro or parsley (for garnish)

Instructions:

1. Rinse the black beans under cold water and remove any debris. Place the beans in a large bowl and cover them with water. Let them soak overnight, or for at least 8 hours.
2. After soaking, drain and rinse the black beans again.
3. In a large pot, heat olive oil over medium heat. Add the chopped onion and bell pepper. Cook until softened, about 5 minutes.
4. Add the minced garlic to the pot and cook for another minute until fragrant.
5. Stir in the drained black beans, ground cumin, dried oregano, salt, pepper, and bay leaf. Cook for a few minutes to toast the spices.
6. Add the water to the pot and bring the mixture to a boil. Reduce the heat to low, cover the pot, and let the beans simmer gently for about 1 to 1.5 hours, or until the beans are tender.
7. Once the beans are tender, stir in the tomato paste and mix well to combine.
8. Add the rice to the pot and stir to combine with the beans. If needed, add more water to ensure the rice is fully submerged.
9. Cover the pot and let the rice and beans simmer over low heat for about 20-25 minutes, or until the rice is cooked through and has absorbed most of the liquid.

10. Once the rice is cooked, remove the pot from the heat and let it sit, covered, for 5-10 minutes to steam.
11. Fluff the rice and beans with a fork, and remove the bay leaf.
12. Serve the Cuban-Style Congri hot, garnished with chopped fresh cilantro or parsley.
13. Enjoy your flavorful and comforting Congri as a delicious side dish or main course!

Cuban-Style Chicken and Rice (Arroz con Pollo)

Ingredients:

- 4 chicken thighs, bone-in and skin-on
- 4 chicken drumsticks, bone-in and skin-on
- Salt and pepper to taste
- 2 tablespoons olive oil
- 1 onion, finely chopped
- 1 bell pepper (red or green), finely chopped
- 2 cloves garlic, minced
- 1 tomato, diced
- 1 teaspoon ground cumin
- 1 teaspoon dried oregano
- 1/2 teaspoon smoked paprika
- 1 cup long-grain white rice
- 2 cups chicken broth
- 1 cup frozen peas
- 1/4 cup chopped fresh cilantro or parsley (for garnish)
- Lemon wedges (for serving)

Instructions:

1. Season the chicken thighs and drumsticks with salt and pepper on both sides.
2. In a large skillet or Dutch oven, heat olive oil over medium-high heat. Add the chicken pieces to the skillet, skin-side down, and cook until golden brown, about 5 minutes per side. Remove the chicken from the skillet and set it aside.
3. In the same skillet, add the chopped onion and bell pepper. Cook until softened, about 5 minutes.
4. Add the minced garlic to the skillet and cook for another minute until fragrant.
5. Stir in the diced tomato, ground cumin, dried oregano, and smoked paprika. Cook for 2-3 minutes until the tomatoes are softened.
6. Add the rice to the skillet and stir to coat it with the vegetable mixture.
7. Pour in the chicken broth and bring the mixture to a simmer.
8. Return the browned chicken pieces to the skillet, nestling them into the rice mixture.

9. Cover the skillet and let the chicken and rice simmer over low heat for about 20-25 minutes, or until the chicken is cooked through and the rice is tender, stirring occasionally.
10. During the last 5 minutes of cooking, add the frozen peas to the skillet and stir to combine.
11. Once the chicken is cooked and the rice is tender, remove the skillet from the heat.
12. Garnish the Cuban-Style Chicken and Rice with chopped fresh cilantro or parsley.
13. Serve the Arroz con Pollo hot, accompanied by lemon wedges for squeezing over the chicken and rice.
14. Enjoy your flavorful and comforting Cuban-style Chicken and Rice!

Cuban-Style Pork Chops (Chuletas de Puerco)

Ingredients:

- 4 pork chops, bone-in or boneless
- Salt and pepper to taste
- 2 tablespoons olive oil
- 1 onion, thinly sliced
- 2 cloves garlic, minced
- 1 bell pepper (red or green), thinly sliced
- 1 tomato, diced
- 1 teaspoon ground cumin
- 1 teaspoon dried oregano
- 1/2 teaspoon smoked paprika
- 1/4 cup orange juice
- 1/4 cup chicken broth or water
- Chopped fresh cilantro or parsley for garnish (optional)
- Lemon wedges for serving (optional)

Instructions:

1. Season the pork chops generously with salt and pepper on both sides.
2. In a large skillet or frying pan, heat olive oil over medium-high heat. Add the pork chops to the skillet and cook until golden brown on both sides, about 4-5 minutes per side. Remove the pork chops from the skillet and set them aside.
3. In the same skillet, add the sliced onion and bell pepper. Cook until softened, about 5 minutes.
4. Add the minced garlic to the skillet and cook for another minute until fragrant.
5. Stir in the diced tomato, ground cumin, dried oregano, and smoked paprika. Cook for 2-3 minutes until the tomatoes are softened and the spices are fragrant.
6. Return the browned pork chops to the skillet, nestling them into the vegetable mixture.
7. Pour in the orange juice and chicken broth (or water) to the skillet. Bring the mixture to a simmer.
8. Reduce the heat to low, cover the skillet, and let the pork chops simmer for about 15-20 minutes, or until they are cooked through and tender, stirring occasionally.
9. Once the pork chops are cooked, remove the skillet from the heat.

10. Garnish the Cuban-Style Pork Chops with chopped fresh cilantro or parsley, if desired.
11. Serve the Chuletas de Puerco hot, accompanied by lemon wedges for squeezing over the pork chops, and your favorite side dishes such as rice, beans, or plantains.
12. Enjoy your flavorful and tender Cuban-style Pork Chops!

Cuban-Style Black Bean Stew (Potaje de Frijoles Negros)

Ingredients:

- 2 cups dried black beans
- 8 cups water
- 2 tablespoons olive oil
- 1 onion, finely chopped
- 1 bell pepper (red or green), finely chopped
- 2 cloves garlic, minced
- 1 tomato, diced
- 1 teaspoon ground cumin
- 1 teaspoon dried oregano
- 1/2 teaspoon smoked paprika
- Salt and pepper to taste
- 1 bay leaf
- 1 cup diced ham or cooked bacon (optional)
- 1 tablespoon white vinegar
- Chopped fresh cilantro or parsley for garnish (optional)
- Cooked white rice for serving

Instructions:

1. Rinse the dried black beans under cold water and remove any debris. Place the beans in a large bowl and cover them with water. Let them soak overnight, or for at least 8 hours.
2. After soaking, drain and rinse the black beans again.
3. In a large pot or Dutch oven, heat olive oil over medium heat. Add the chopped onion and bell pepper. Cook until softened, about 5 minutes.
4. Add the minced garlic to the pot and cook for another minute until fragrant.
5. Stir in the diced tomato, ground cumin, dried oregano, and smoked paprika. Cook for 2-3 minutes until the tomatoes are softened and the spices are fragrant.
6. Add the soaked black beans to the pot, along with the 8 cups of water and the bay leaf. If using diced ham or cooked bacon, add it to the pot as well.
7. Bring the mixture to a boil, then reduce the heat to low. Cover the pot and let the stew simmer gently for about 1 to 1.5 hours, or until the beans are tender, stirring occasionally.

8. Once the beans are tender, stir in the white vinegar and season the stew with salt and pepper to taste. Adjust the seasoning as needed.
9. Remove the bay leaf from the pot.
10. If desired, use an immersion blender to partially blend some of the beans and vegetables in the stew to thicken it slightly. Alternatively, you can remove a portion of the stew and blend it in a blender or food processor, then return it to the pot.
11. Serve the Cuban-Style Black Bean Stew hot, garnished with chopped fresh cilantro or parsley, if desired.
12. Serve with cooked white rice on the side.
13. Enjoy your hearty and flavorful Potaje de Frijoles Negros!

Cuban-Style Chicken Salad (Ensalada de Pollo)

Ingredients:

For the chicken:

- 2 boneless, skinless chicken breasts
- Salt and pepper to taste
- 1 tablespoon olive oil

For the salad:

- 4 cups mixed salad greens (such as lettuce, spinach, and arugula)
- 1 cucumber, thinly sliced
- 1 bell pepper (red or green), thinly sliced
- 1 tomato, diced
- 1/2 red onion, thinly sliced
- 1 avocado, diced
- 1/4 cup chopped fresh cilantro or parsley (optional, for garnish)

For the dressing:

- 1/4 cup olive oil
- 2 tablespoons lime juice
- 1 tablespoon white vinegar
- 1 teaspoon honey or sugar
- 1 teaspoon Dijon mustard
- 1 clove garlic, minced
- Salt and pepper to taste

Instructions:

1. Season the chicken breasts with salt and pepper on both sides.

2. In a skillet, heat olive oil over medium-high heat. Add the seasoned chicken breasts to the skillet and cook until golden brown on both sides and cooked through, about 6-8 minutes per side.
3. Remove the cooked chicken from the skillet and let it rest for a few minutes. Once cooled, slice the chicken into thin strips or cubes.
4. In a large salad bowl, combine the mixed salad greens, sliced cucumber, sliced bell pepper, diced tomato, sliced red onion, and diced avocado.
5. Add the sliced or cubed chicken to the salad bowl.
6. In a small bowl, whisk together the olive oil, lime juice, white vinegar, honey or sugar, Dijon mustard, minced garlic, salt, and pepper to make the dressing.
7. Pour the dressing over the salad ingredients in the bowl.
8. Gently toss the salad until all ingredients are evenly coated with the dressing.
9. Garnish the Cuban-Style Chicken Salad with chopped fresh cilantro or parsley, if desired.
10. Serve the Ensalada de Pollo immediately as a refreshing and satisfying meal.
11. Enjoy your flavorful and zesty Cuban-style Chicken Salad!

Cuban-Style Stuffed Avocado (Aguacate Relleno)

Ingredients:

- 2 ripe avocados
- 1 cup cooked shrimp, chopped
- 1/2 cup cooked crab meat or imitation crab, chopped
- 1/4 cup red onion, finely chopped
- 1/4 cup red bell pepper, finely chopped
- 1/4 cup cucumber, finely chopped
- 2 tablespoons fresh cilantro, chopped
- 2 tablespoons mayonnaise
- 1 tablespoon lime juice
- Salt and pepper to taste
- Dash of hot sauce (optional)
- Lettuce leaves, for serving
- Lime wedges, for garnish

Instructions:

1. Cut the ripe avocados in half lengthwise and remove the pits. Scoop out some of the flesh from each avocado half to create a larger cavity for stuffing, leaving a border around the edge.
2. In a mixing bowl, combine the chopped shrimp, crab meat, red onion, red bell pepper, cucumber, and fresh cilantro.
3. In a separate small bowl, whisk together the mayonnaise, lime juice, salt, pepper, and hot sauce (if using).
4. Pour the mayonnaise mixture over the shrimp and crab mixture and toss until everything is well combined and evenly coated.
5. Spoon the shrimp and crab mixture into the hollowed-out avocado halves, dividing it evenly among them.
6. Place the stuffed avocado halves on a bed of lettuce leaves on a serving platter.
7. Garnish the stuffed avocados with additional chopped cilantro and lime wedges.
8. Serve the Cuban-Style Stuffed Avocado as a delicious appetizer or light meal.
9. Enjoy your flavorful and satisfying Aguacate Relleno!

Cuban-Style Pork Sandwich (Pan con Lechón)

Ingredients:

For the roasted pork:

- 2 lbs pork shoulder (or pork loin)
- 4 cloves garlic, minced
- 1 teaspoon dried oregano
- 1 teaspoon ground cumin
- 1 teaspoon salt
- 1/2 teaspoon black pepper
- 1/4 cup orange juice
- 1/4 cup lime juice
- 2 tablespoons olive oil

For the sandwich:

- Cuban bread or French bread, sliced lengthwise
- Roasted pork (prepared according to the recipe above)
- Mojo sauce (see recipe below)
- Sliced onions (marinated in lime juice, salt, and pepper)
- Sliced pickles (optional)
- Mustard (optional)
- Butter or olive oil (for grilling or toasting the bread)

For the mojo sauce:

- 1/4 cup olive oil
- 4 cloves garlic, minced
- 1/4 cup orange juice
- 1/4 cup lime juice
- 1 teaspoon dried oregano
- Salt and pepper to taste

Instructions:

1. Preheat the oven to 325°F (165°C).
2. In a small bowl, mix together the minced garlic, dried oregano, ground cumin, salt, pepper, orange juice, lime juice, and olive oil to make the marinade for the pork.
3. Place the pork shoulder (or pork loin) in a roasting pan or baking dish. Pour the marinade over the pork, making sure it's evenly coated. Cover the pan with aluminum foil and let it marinate in the refrigerator for at least 1 hour, or preferably overnight.
4. Roast the marinated pork in the preheated oven for 2.5 to 3 hours, or until it's tender and easily shreds with a fork. Remove the foil during the last 30 minutes of cooking to allow the pork to brown.
5. While the pork is roasting, prepare the mojo sauce. In a small saucepan, heat the olive oil over medium heat. Add the minced garlic and cook until fragrant, about 1 minute. Stir in the orange juice, lime juice, dried oregano, salt, and pepper. Simmer for 2-3 minutes, then remove from heat and set aside.
6. Once the pork is cooked, remove it from the oven and let it rest for a few minutes. Then, shred the pork using two forks.
7. To assemble the sandwiches, spread a layer of mojo sauce on the bottom half of each sliced Cuban bread or French bread. Place a generous amount of shredded pork on top of the sauce.
8. Top the pork with sliced onions (marinated in lime juice, salt, and pepper), pickles (if using), and mustard (if desired). Close the sandwiches with the top half of the bread.
9. Heat a skillet or griddle over medium heat. Spread butter or olive oil on the outside of each sandwich. Place the sandwiches on the skillet or griddle and cook until the bread is golden brown and crispy, and the filling is heated through, about 3-4 minutes per side.
10. Serve the Cuban-Style Pork Sandwiches hot, with additional mojo sauce on the side for dipping, if desired.
11. Enjoy your delicious and authentic Pan con Lechón!

Cuban-Style Fish Tacos (Tacos de Pescado)

Ingredients:

For the fish:

- 1 lb white fish fillets (such as tilapia, cod, or mahi-mahi)
- 2 tablespoons olive oil
- 1 teaspoon ground cumin
- 1 teaspoon paprika
- 1/2 teaspoon garlic powder
- Salt and pepper to taste
- Juice of 1 lime

For the cabbage slaw:

- 2 cups shredded cabbage (green or purple)
- 1 carrot, grated
- 1/4 cup chopped fresh cilantro
- 2 tablespoons mayonnaise
- 1 tablespoon lime juice
- Salt and pepper to taste

For serving:

- 8 small corn or flour tortillas
- Sliced avocado
- Sliced jalapeños
- Lime wedges
- Chopped fresh cilantro

Instructions:

1. Preheat the oven to 375°F (190°C).

2. In a small bowl, mix together the olive oil, ground cumin, paprika, garlic powder, salt, pepper, and lime juice to make a marinade for the fish.
3. Place the fish fillets in a baking dish and pour the marinade over them, making sure they are evenly coated. Let them marinate for about 15-30 minutes.
4. While the fish is marinating, prepare the cabbage slaw. In a large bowl, combine the shredded cabbage, grated carrot, chopped cilantro, mayonnaise, lime juice, salt, and pepper. Toss until everything is well combined and the cabbage is coated with the dressing. Refrigerate until ready to use.
5. After the fish has marinated, bake it in the preheated oven for about 15-20 minutes, or until it's cooked through and flakes easily with a fork.
6. While the fish is baking, warm the tortillas in a dry skillet or in the oven.
7. Once the fish is cooked, remove it from the oven and let it cool slightly. Then, flake the fish into bite-sized pieces using a fork.
8. To assemble the tacos, place some flaked fish on each warmed tortilla. Top with a generous portion of the cabbage slaw, sliced avocado, and sliced jalapeños. Garnish with lime wedges and chopped cilantro.
9. Serve the Cuban-Style Fish Tacos immediately, with additional lime wedges on the side for squeezing over the tacos, if desired.
10. Enjoy your flavorful and vibrant Tacos de Pescado!

Cuban-Style Shrimp and Rice (Arroz con Camarones)

Ingredients:

- 1 lb large shrimp, peeled and deveined
- 2 cups long-grain white rice
- 4 cups chicken broth or seafood broth
- 2 tablespoons olive oil
- 1 onion, finely chopped
- 1 bell pepper (red or green), finely chopped
- 2 cloves garlic, minced
- 1 tomato, diced
- 1 teaspoon ground cumin
- 1 teaspoon dried oregano
- 1/2 teaspoon smoked paprika
- Salt and pepper to taste
- 1/4 cup chopped fresh cilantro or parsley (for garnish)
- Lime wedges for serving

Instructions:

1. Rinse the rice under cold water until the water runs clear. Drain well and set aside.
2. In a large skillet or Dutch oven, heat olive oil over medium heat. Add the chopped onion and bell pepper. Cook until softened, about 5 minutes.
3. Add the minced garlic to the skillet and cook for another minute until fragrant.
4. Stir in the diced tomato, ground cumin, dried oregano, and smoked paprika. Cook for 2-3 minutes until the tomatoes are softened and the spices are fragrant.
5. Add the rinsed rice to the skillet and stir to coat it with the vegetable mixture.
6. Pour in the chicken broth or seafood broth and bring the mixture to a simmer.
7. Reduce the heat to low, cover the skillet, and let the rice simmer for about 15-20 minutes, or until the rice is almost cooked through and most of the liquid has been absorbed.
8. While the rice is cooking, season the shrimp with salt and pepper to taste.
9. Once the rice is almost cooked, arrange the seasoned shrimp on top of the rice in an even layer.

10. Cover the skillet again and let the shrimp cook for about 5-7 minutes, or until they are pink and opaque.
11. Once the shrimp are cooked through and the rice is tender, remove the skillet from the heat.
12. Garnish the Cuban-Style Shrimp and Rice with chopped fresh cilantro or parsley.
13. Serve the Arroz con Camarones hot, accompanied by lime wedges for squeezing over the dish.
14. Enjoy your flavorful and aromatic Cuban-style Shrimp and Rice!

Cuban-Style Beef Stir-Fry (Bistec Salteado)

Ingredients:

- 1 lb flank steak or sirloin steak, thinly sliced against the grain
- 2 tablespoons olive oil
- 1 onion, thinly sliced
- 1 bell pepper (red or green), thinly sliced
- 2 cloves garlic, minced
- 1 tomato, diced
- 2 tablespoons soy sauce
- 1 tablespoon lime juice
- 1 teaspoon ground cumin
- 1 teaspoon dried oregano
- 1/2 teaspoon smoked paprika
- Salt and pepper to taste
- Chopped fresh cilantro or parsley for garnish
- Cooked white rice for serving

Instructions:

1. In a small bowl, combine the soy sauce, lime juice, ground cumin, dried oregano, smoked paprika, salt, and pepper. Mix well to make the marinade.
2. Place the thinly sliced beef in a shallow dish and pour the marinade over it, making sure all the beef is evenly coated. Let it marinate for at least 30 minutes, or preferably for a few hours in the refrigerator.
3. Heat 1 tablespoon of olive oil in a large skillet or wok over medium-high heat. Add the marinated beef to the skillet and stir-fry for 2-3 minutes, or until browned and cooked through. Remove the beef from the skillet and set it aside.
4. In the same skillet, heat the remaining tablespoon of olive oil over medium heat. Add the thinly sliced onion and bell pepper to the skillet. Cook until softened, about 5 minutes.
5. Add the minced garlic to the skillet and cook for another minute until fragrant.
6. Stir in the diced tomato and cooked beef. Cook for 2-3 minutes, stirring occasionally, until everything is heated through.
7. Taste and adjust the seasoning with salt and pepper if needed.

8. Serve the Cuban-Style Beef Stir-Fry (Bistec Salteado) hot, garnished with chopped fresh cilantro or parsley.
9. Serve the stir-fry over cooked white rice.
10. Enjoy your delicious and flavorful Bistec Salteado as a satisfying meal!

Cuban-Style Vegetable Soup (Sopa de Verduras)

Ingredients:

- 2 tablespoons olive oil
- 1 onion, diced
- 2 cloves garlic, minced
- 2 carrots, diced
- 2 celery stalks, diced
- 1 bell pepper (red or green), diced
- 1 zucchini, diced
- 1 yellow squash, diced
- 1 potato, peeled and diced
- 1 tomato, diced
- 6 cups vegetable broth or chicken broth
- 1 teaspoon ground cumin
- 1 teaspoon dried oregano
- 1/2 teaspoon smoked paprika
- Salt and pepper to taste
- 2 cups chopped kale or spinach
- 1/4 cup chopped fresh cilantro or parsley
- Lime wedges for serving

Instructions:

1. In a large pot or Dutch oven, heat the olive oil over medium heat. Add the diced onion and cook until softened, about 5 minutes.
2. Add the minced garlic to the pot and cook for another minute until fragrant.
3. Stir in the diced carrots, celery, bell pepper, zucchini, yellow squash, and potato. Cook for 5-7 minutes, stirring occasionally, until the vegetables start to soften.
4. Add the diced tomato to the pot and cook for another 2-3 minutes.
5. Pour in the vegetable broth or chicken broth and bring the mixture to a simmer.
6. Stir in the ground cumin, dried oregano, smoked paprika, salt, and pepper to taste.
7. Let the soup simmer for about 15-20 minutes, or until the vegetables are tender.
8. Add the chopped kale or spinach to the pot and cook for another 2-3 minutes, until wilted.

9. Taste and adjust the seasoning with salt and pepper if needed.
10. Remove the pot from the heat and stir in the chopped fresh cilantro or parsley.
11. Serve the Cuban-Style Vegetable Soup hot, with lime wedges on the side for squeezing over the soup, if desired.
12. Enjoy your comforting and flavorful Sopa de Verduras!

Cuban-Style Crab Cakes (Pastelitos de Cangrejo)

Ingredients:

- 1 lb lump crab meat, drained and picked over for shells
- 1/2 cup breadcrumbs
- 1/4 cup mayonnaise
- 1 egg, lightly beaten
- 2 tablespoons chopped fresh cilantro or parsley
- 2 green onions, thinly sliced
- 1 tablespoon lime juice
- 1 teaspoon Dijon mustard
- 1 teaspoon Worcestershire sauce
- 1/2 teaspoon smoked paprika
- 1/4 teaspoon cayenne pepper (optional)
- Salt and pepper to taste
- 2 tablespoons olive oil, for frying

For the remoulade sauce (optional):

- 1/2 cup mayonnaise
- 2 tablespoons chopped pickles or pickle relish
- 1 tablespoon chopped fresh cilantro or parsley
- 1 tablespoon lime juice
- 1 teaspoon Dijon mustard
- 1/2 teaspoon smoked paprika
- Salt and pepper to taste

Instructions:

1. In a large mixing bowl, combine the lump crab meat, breadcrumbs, mayonnaise, beaten egg, chopped cilantro or parsley, sliced green onions, lime juice, Dijon mustard, Worcestershire sauce, smoked paprika, cayenne pepper (if using), salt, and pepper. Gently mix until all ingredients are well combined.
2. Divide the crab mixture into equal portions and shape them into round patties.

3. Heat the olive oil in a large skillet over medium heat. Once the oil is hot, carefully place the crab cakes in the skillet, making sure not to overcrowd the pan.
4. Cook the crab cakes for 3-4 minutes on each side, or until they are golden brown and crispy on the outside and heated through.
5. While the crab cakes are cooking, prepare the remoulade sauce (if using). In a small bowl, combine the mayonnaise, chopped pickles or pickle relish, chopped cilantro or parsley, lime juice, Dijon mustard, smoked paprika, salt, and pepper. Mix well until smooth and creamy.
6. Once the crab cakes are cooked, transfer them to a plate lined with paper towels to drain any excess oil.
7. Serve the Cuban-Style Crab Cakes hot, garnished with chopped fresh cilantro or parsley, and with the remoulade sauce on the side for dipping, if desired.
8. Enjoy your delicious and flavorful Pastelitos de Cangrejo as an appetizer or main dish!

Cuban-Style Beef Skewers (Pinchos de Carne)

Ingredients:

For the marinade:

- 1/4 cup olive oil
- 2 tablespoons lime juice
- 2 cloves garlic, minced
- 1 teaspoon ground cumin
- 1 teaspoon dried oregano
- 1/2 teaspoon smoked paprika
- 1/2 teaspoon salt
- 1/4 teaspoon black pepper

For the skewers:

- 1 lb beef sirloin or flank steak, cut into 1-inch cubes
- 1 onion, cut into chunks
- 1 bell pepper (red or green), cut into chunks
- Cherry tomatoes
- Wooden skewers, soaked in water for at least 30 minutes

Instructions:

1. In a small bowl, whisk together the olive oil, lime juice, minced garlic, ground cumin, dried oregano, smoked paprika, salt, and black pepper to make the marinade.
2. Place the cubed beef in a shallow dish or resealable plastic bag. Pour the marinade over the beef, making sure it's evenly coated. Cover the dish or seal the bag and refrigerate for at least 1 hour, or preferably overnight, to allow the flavors to meld.
3. Preheat the grill to medium-high heat.
4. Thread the marinated beef cubes onto the soaked wooden skewers, alternating with chunks of onion, bell pepper, and cherry tomatoes.

5. Once the grill is hot, place the skewers on the grill grates. Cook for 3-4 minutes per side, or until the beef is cooked to your desired level of doneness and the vegetables are charred and tender.
6. Remove the skewers from the grill and transfer them to a serving platter.
7. Serve the Cuban-Style Beef Skewers hot, garnished with chopped fresh cilantro or parsley if desired.
8. Enjoy your flavorful and delicious Pinchos de Carne as a main dish or appetizer!

Cuban-Style Chicken and Plantains (Pollo con Plátanos)

Ingredients:

- 4 bone-in, skin-on chicken thighs
- Salt and pepper to taste
- 2 tablespoons olive oil
- 2 ripe plantains, peeled and sliced diagonally into 1-inch pieces
- 1 onion, chopped
- 2 cloves garlic, minced
- 1 bell pepper (red or green), chopped
- 1 tomato, diced
- 1 teaspoon ground cumin
- 1 teaspoon dried oregano
- 1/2 teaspoon smoked paprika
- 1 cup chicken broth
- 1/4 cup orange juice
- 2 tablespoons lime juice
- Chopped fresh cilantro or parsley for garnish

Instructions:

1. Season the chicken thighs with salt and pepper on both sides.
2. In a large skillet or Dutch oven, heat the olive oil over medium-high heat. Add the chicken thighs to the skillet, skin side down. Cook until the skin is golden brown and crispy, about 5-6 minutes. Flip the chicken thighs and cook for another 5-6 minutes on the other side. Remove the chicken from the skillet and set it aside.
3. In the same skillet, add the sliced plantains. Cook until they are golden brown on both sides, about 2-3 minutes per side. Remove the plantains from the skillet and set them aside.
4. Add the chopped onion, minced garlic, and chopped bell pepper to the skillet. Cook until the vegetables are softened, about 5 minutes.
5. Stir in the diced tomato, ground cumin, dried oregano, and smoked paprika. Cook for another 2-3 minutes until the tomatoes are softened and the spices are fragrant.
6. Return the chicken thighs to the skillet, nestling them into the vegetable mixture.

7. Pour in the chicken broth, orange juice, and lime juice. Bring the mixture to a simmer.
8. Reduce the heat to low, cover the skillet, and let the chicken simmer for about 20-25 minutes, or until it's cooked through and tender, and the sauce has thickened slightly.
9. Once the chicken is cooked, add the cooked plantains back to the skillet, arranging them around the chicken pieces.
10. Allow the chicken and plantains to simmer together in the sauce for another 5 minutes to heat through and absorb the flavors.
11. Garnish the Cuban-Style Chicken and Plantains with chopped fresh cilantro or parsley before serving.
12. Serve the Pollo con Plátanos hot, accompanied by rice or your favorite side dish.
13. Enjoy your delicious and flavorful Cuban-style chicken and plantains!

Cuban-Style Stuffed Tomatoes (Tomates Rellenos)

Ingredients:

- 4 large ripe tomatoes
- 1 cup cooked white rice
- 1/2 lb ground beef or turkey
- 1 onion, finely chopped
- 2 cloves garlic, minced
- 1 bell pepper (red or green), finely chopped
- 1/4 cup tomato sauce
- 1 teaspoon ground cumin
- 1 teaspoon dried oregano
- Salt and pepper to taste
- 1/4 cup grated Parmesan cheese (optional)
- Chopped fresh parsley for garnish

Instructions:

1. Preheat the oven to 375°F (190°C).
2. Cut the tops off the tomatoes and carefully scoop out the seeds and pulp with a spoon, leaving the tomato shells intact. Reserve the pulp for later use.
3. In a skillet, cook the ground beef or turkey over medium heat until browned. Drain any excess fat.
4. Add the chopped onion, minced garlic, and chopped bell pepper to the skillet with the cooked meat. Cook until the vegetables are softened, about 5 minutes.
5. Stir in the cooked white rice, tomato sauce, ground cumin, dried oregano, salt, and pepper. Cook for another 2-3 minutes until everything is well combined and heated through.
6. If desired, add the reserved tomato pulp to the skillet and cook for an additional 2-3 minutes to incorporate the flavors.
7. Stuff each hollowed-out tomato with the rice and meat mixture, pressing it down gently to fill the cavity.
8. Place the stuffed tomatoes in a baking dish. If desired, sprinkle grated Parmesan cheese on top of each tomato.
9. Bake in the preheated oven for 20-25 minutes, or until the tomatoes are tender and the filling is heated through.

10. Garnish the Cuban-Style Stuffed Tomatoes with chopped fresh parsley before serving.
11. Serve the Tomates Rellenos hot as a delicious side dish or light meal.
12. Enjoy your flavorful and satisfying Cuban-style stuffed tomatoes!

Cuban-Style Seafood Salad (Ensalada de Mariscos)

Ingredients:

For the salad:

- 1 lb mixed seafood (shrimp, calamari, scallops, etc.), cooked and cooled
- 1 cucumber, diced
- 1 bell pepper (red or green), diced
- 1 tomato, diced
- 1/4 cup red onion, thinly sliced
- 1/4 cup chopped fresh cilantro or parsley
- 1 avocado, diced (optional)
- Lettuce leaves for serving

For the dressing:

- 1/4 cup olive oil
- 2 tablespoons lime juice
- 1 tablespoon white vinegar
- 1 clove garlic, minced
- 1 teaspoon Dijon mustard
- 1 teaspoon honey or sugar
- Salt and pepper to taste

Instructions:

1. In a large salad bowl, combine the cooked and cooled seafood, diced cucumber, diced bell pepper, diced tomato, thinly sliced red onion, chopped fresh cilantro or parsley, and diced avocado (if using).
2. In a small bowl, whisk together the olive oil, lime juice, white vinegar, minced garlic, Dijon mustard, honey or sugar, salt, and pepper to make the dressing.
3. Pour the dressing over the seafood and vegetable mixture in the salad bowl. Toss gently until all ingredients are evenly coated with the dressing.
4. Place lettuce leaves on serving plates or in a large serving bowl.
5. Spoon the Cuban-Style Seafood Salad onto the lettuce leaves.

6. Garnish the salad with additional chopped fresh cilantro or parsley if desired.
7. Serve the Ensalada de Mariscos immediately as a refreshing and satisfying appetizer or light meal.
8. Enjoy your flavorful and zesty Cuban-style seafood salad!

Cuban-Style Grilled Chicken (Pollo a la Parrilla)

Ingredients:

- 4 boneless, skinless chicken breasts
- 1/4 cup olive oil
- 2 tablespoons lime juice
- 2 cloves garlic, minced
- 1 teaspoon ground cumin
- 1 teaspoon dried oregano
- 1/2 teaspoon smoked paprika
- Salt and pepper to taste
- Chopped fresh cilantro or parsley for garnish
- Lime wedges for serving

Instructions:

1. In a small bowl, whisk together the olive oil, lime juice, minced garlic, ground cumin, dried oregano, smoked paprika, salt, and pepper to make the marinade.
2. Place the chicken breasts in a shallow dish or resealable plastic bag. Pour the marinade over the chicken, making sure each piece is evenly coated. Cover the dish or seal the bag and refrigerate for at least 30 minutes, or up to 4 hours, to allow the flavors to meld.
3. Preheat the grill to medium-high heat.
4. Remove the chicken from the marinade and discard any excess marinade.
5. Place the chicken breasts on the preheated grill. Grill for 6-8 minutes per side, or until the chicken is cooked through and no longer pink in the center, and grill marks appear.
6. Remove the grilled chicken from the grill and let it rest for a few minutes before serving.
7. Garnish the Cuban-Style Grilled Chicken with chopped fresh cilantro or parsley.
8. Serve the Pollo a la Parrilla hot, accompanied by lime wedges for squeezing over the chicken, if desired.
9. Enjoy your flavorful and juicy Cuban-style grilled chicken!

Cuban-Style Beef Tamales (Tamales de Carne)

Ingredients:

For the beef filling:

- 1 lb ground beef
- 1 onion, finely chopped
- 2 cloves garlic, minced
- 1 bell pepper (red or green), finely chopped
- 1 tomato, diced
- 1 teaspoon ground cumin
- 1 teaspoon dried oregano
- 1/2 teaspoon smoked paprika
- Salt and pepper to taste
- 1/4 cup chopped fresh cilantro or parsley

For the corn masa dough:

- 2 cups masa harina (corn flour)
- 1 1/2 cups chicken broth or water
- 1/2 cup vegetable shortening or lard
- 1 teaspoon baking powder
- Salt to taste

For assembling:

- Dried corn husks, soaked in warm water for at least 30 minutes
- Kitchen twine or strips of corn husks for tying

Instructions:

1. To make the beef filling, heat a skillet over medium heat. Add the ground beef and cook until browned, breaking it apart with a spoon. Drain any excess fat.

2. Add the chopped onion, minced garlic, chopped bell pepper, and diced tomato to the skillet with the cooked beef. Cook until the vegetables are softened, about 5 minutes.
3. Stir in the ground cumin, dried oregano, smoked paprika, salt, and pepper. Cook for another 2-3 minutes until the spices are fragrant.
4. Remove the skillet from the heat and stir in the chopped fresh cilantro or parsley. Set aside the beef filling to cool slightly.
5. To make the corn masa dough, in a large mixing bowl, combine the masa harina, chicken broth or water, vegetable shortening or lard, baking powder, and salt. Mix until a soft dough forms. If the dough is too dry, add more broth or water, 1 tablespoon at a time, until the desired consistency is reached.
6. To assemble the tamales, pat dry a soaked corn husk with a clean kitchen towel. Spread a thin layer of the corn masa dough onto the wide end of the husk, leaving a border around the edges.
7. Spoon a small amount of the beef filling onto the center of the masa dough.
8. Fold one side of the corn husk over the filling, then fold the other side to enclose the filling completely. Fold up the narrow end of the husk to seal the tamale, leaving the other end open.
9. Repeat the process with the remaining corn husks, masa dough, and beef filling.
10. To cook the tamales, arrange them upright in a steamer basket, open ends up. Make sure they are tightly packed together to prevent them from opening during cooking.
11. Steam the tamales over simmering water for 1 1/2 to 2 hours, or until the masa dough is firm and cooked through.
12. Once cooked, remove the tamales from the steamer and let them cool slightly before serving.
13. Serve the Cuban-Style Beef Tamales hot, either as a main dish or as a snack, accompanied by your favorite salsa or sauce.
14. Enjoy your delicious and authentic Tamales de Carne!

Cuban-Style Pork Stew (Cerdo en Salsa)

Ingredients:

- 2 lbs pork shoulder, cut into 1-inch cubes
- Salt and pepper to taste
- 2 tablespoons olive oil
- 1 onion, chopped
- 2 bell peppers (red and green), chopped
- 3 cloves garlic, minced
- 1 teaspoon ground cumin
- 1 teaspoon dried oregano
- 1/2 teaspoon smoked paprika
- 1/4 teaspoon cayenne pepper (optional)
- 1 can (14.5 oz) diced tomatoes
- 1 cup chicken broth or water
- 1/4 cup dry white wine (optional)
- 2 bay leaves
- 1/4 cup chopped fresh cilantro or parsley for garnish

Instructions:

1. Season the pork cubes with salt and pepper to taste.
2. Heat the olive oil in a large Dutch oven or heavy-bottomed pot over medium-high heat. Add the seasoned pork cubes in batches and cook until browned on all sides. Remove the browned pork from the pot and set it aside.
3. In the same pot, add the chopped onion and bell peppers. Cook until softened, about 5 minutes.
4. Add the minced garlic to the pot and cook for another minute until fragrant.
5. Stir in the ground cumin, dried oregano, smoked paprika, and cayenne pepper (if using). Cook for 1-2 minutes until the spices are toasted and fragrant.
6. Return the browned pork cubes to the pot. Add the diced tomatoes (with their juices), chicken broth or water, dry white wine (if using), and bay leaves. Stir to combine.
7. Bring the mixture to a simmer, then reduce the heat to low. Cover the pot and let the stew simmer gently for 1 1/2 to 2 hours, stirring occasionally, until the pork is tender and the sauce has thickened.

8. Taste and adjust the seasoning with salt and pepper if needed.
9. Once the pork is cooked through and tender, remove the pot from the heat.
10. Discard the bay leaves and garnish the Cuban-Style Pork Stew with chopped fresh cilantro or parsley before serving.
11. Serve the Cerdo en Salsa hot, accompanied by rice, mashed potatoes, or your favorite side dish.
12. Enjoy your hearty and flavorful Cuban-style pork stew!

Cuban-Style Stuffed Squash (Calabacitas Rellenas)

Ingredients:

- 4 medium-sized yellow squash or zucchini
- 1 tablespoon olive oil
- 1 onion, diced
- 2 cloves garlic, minced
- 1 bell pepper (red or green), diced
- 1 tomato, diced
- 1 cup cooked rice
- 1 cup cooked black beans
- 1 teaspoon ground cumin
- 1 teaspoon dried oregano
- 1/2 teaspoon smoked paprika
- Salt and pepper to taste
- 1/4 cup chopped fresh cilantro or parsley
- Shredded cheese for topping (optional)

Instructions:

1. Preheat the oven to 375°F (190°C).
2. Cut the squash in half lengthwise and scoop out the seeds and pulp with a spoon, creating a hollow center for the filling. Reserve the squash pulp for later use.
3. Place the squash halves in a baking dish, cut side up.
4. Heat the olive oil in a skillet over medium heat. Add the diced onion, minced garlic, and diced bell pepper to the skillet. Cook until the vegetables are softened, about 5 minutes.
5. Stir in the diced tomato and cook for another 2-3 minutes until the tomatoes are softened.
6. Add the cooked rice, cooked black beans, ground cumin, dried oregano, smoked paprika, salt, and pepper to the skillet. Mix well to combine.
7. Cook for another 2-3 minutes until the filling is heated through and well seasoned.
8. Chop the reserved squash pulp and add it to the skillet. Cook for another 2-3 minutes until the squash is softened and incorporated into the filling mixture.

9. Remove the skillet from the heat and stir in the chopped fresh cilantro or parsley.
10. Spoon the filling mixture into the hollowed-out squash halves, dividing it evenly among them.
11. If desired, sprinkle shredded cheese on top of each stuffed squash half.
12. Cover the baking dish with aluminum foil and bake in the preheated oven for 25-30 minutes, or until the squash is tender and the filling is heated through.
13. Remove the foil and bake for an additional 5-10 minutes, or until the cheese is melted and bubbly (if using).
14. Once cooked, remove the Cuban-Style Stuffed Squash from the oven and let them cool slightly before serving.
15. Serve the Calabacitas Rellenas hot, garnished with additional chopped fresh cilantro or parsley if desired.
16. Enjoy your flavorful and satisfying Cuban-style stuffed squash!

Cuban-Style Beef Ribs (Costillas de Res)

Ingredients:

- 3 lbs beef ribs
- Salt and pepper to taste
- 2 tablespoons olive oil
- 1 onion, chopped
- 4 cloves garlic, minced
- 1 bell pepper (red or green), chopped
- 1 tomato, diced
- 1/4 cup tomato paste
- 1 cup beef broth
- 1/4 cup white wine vinegar
- 2 tablespoons brown sugar
- 1 tablespoon Worcestershire sauce
- 1 teaspoon ground cumin
- 1 teaspoon dried oregano
- 1/2 teaspoon smoked paprika
- 1/4 teaspoon cayenne pepper (optional)
- Chopped fresh cilantro or parsley for garnish

Instructions:

1. Season the beef ribs with salt and pepper to taste.
2. In a large skillet or Dutch oven, heat the olive oil over medium-high heat. Add the beef ribs and cook until browned on all sides. Remove the ribs from the skillet and set them aside.
3. In the same skillet, add the chopped onion, minced garlic, and chopped bell pepper. Cook until the vegetables are softened, about 5 minutes.
4. Stir in the diced tomato and cook for another 2-3 minutes.
5. Add the tomato paste to the skillet and cook for 1-2 minutes, stirring constantly.
6. Pour in the beef broth, white wine vinegar, brown sugar, Worcestershire sauce, ground cumin, dried oregano, smoked paprika, and cayenne pepper (if using). Stir to combine.
7. Return the browned beef ribs to the skillet, nestling them into the sauce.

8. Bring the mixture to a simmer, then reduce the heat to low. Cover the skillet and let the beef ribs simmer gently for 2-3 hours, or until the meat is tender and falling off the bone.
9. Once the beef ribs are cooked through and tender, remove them from the skillet and place them on a serving platter.
10. Spoon the Cuban-Style Beef Ribs sauce over the ribs, garnish with chopped fresh cilantro or parsley, and serve hot.
11. Enjoy your flavorful and succulent Costillas de Res with your favorite side dishes!

Cuban-Style Seafood Stew (Estofado de Mariscos)

Ingredients:

- 1 lb mixed seafood (shrimp, fish fillets, scallops, mussels, etc.)
- 2 tablespoons olive oil
- 1 onion, chopped
- 2 cloves garlic, minced
- 1 bell pepper (red or green), chopped
- 1 tomato, diced
- 1/4 cup tomato paste
- 2 cups seafood broth or fish stock
- 1 cup dry white wine
- 1 teaspoon ground cumin
- 1 teaspoon dried oregano
- 1/2 teaspoon smoked paprika
- Salt and pepper to taste
- 1/4 cup chopped fresh cilantro or parsley for garnish
- Lime wedges for serving

Instructions:

1. Heat the olive oil in a large pot or Dutch oven over medium heat. Add the chopped onion, minced garlic, and chopped bell pepper. Cook until the vegetables are softened, about 5 minutes.
2. Stir in the diced tomato and tomato paste. Cook for another 2-3 minutes.
3. Add the seafood broth or fish stock and dry white wine to the pot. Bring the mixture to a simmer.
4. Stir in the ground cumin, dried oregano, smoked paprika, salt, and pepper to taste.
5. Once the broth is simmering, add the mixed seafood to the pot. Stir gently to combine.
6. Cover the pot and let the seafood stew simmer for about 10-15 minutes, or until the seafood is cooked through and tender.
7. Taste and adjust the seasoning with salt and pepper if needed.
8. Once the seafood is cooked, remove the pot from the heat.

9. Ladle the Cuban-Style Seafood Stew into bowls and garnish with chopped fresh cilantro or parsley.
10. Serve the Estofado de Mariscos hot, with lime wedges on the side for squeezing over the stew, if desired.
11. Enjoy your flavorful and comforting Cuban-style seafood stew!